POSITIVE CHRISTIAN AFFIRMATIONS AND TRUSTING GOD

One Year Journal and Devotional

POSITIVE CHRISTIAN AFFIRMATIONS AND TRUSTING GOD

One Year Journal and Devotional

NANCY M. STRONG

Positive Christian Affirmations and Trusting God
by Nancy M. Strong

Cover Design by Atinad Designs.

© Copyright 2015

SAINT PAUL PRESS, DALLAS, TEXAS

First Printing, 2015

Second Printing, 2017

ISBN-13: 978-0996324106
ISBN-10: 0996324100

Printed in the U.S.A.

DEDICATION

This book is dedicated to:

God's Angels who are with us always;

Pastor Lou Butler for his words of wisdom, and his wife, Connie, who proof read this book;

Pastor Jerry Rittenhouse and Rev. Jim Rhea who gave so much encouragement;

My brother, Steve, and his wife, Debby, and their family who have stood by me;

My five children and their families whom I love very much;

And to my closest friends who mean so much to me.

CONTENTS

FROM THE AUTHOR

My inspiration to write this book, *Positive Christian Affirmations and Trusting God,* came after a near death experience from a pulmonary embolism in 2001. This out of body episode, along with seeing angels who left my side gradually disappearing in a few seconds, gave me a whole new outlook on life. I can still relax just by remembering the voice of the angel that was holding my right arm when she told me to "relax" moments before she left my side.

This book combines my experience as a mother of five children who are all college graduates and includes our travels all over the United States, parts of Canada, and parts of Mexico. Included in this book are my experiences with having an Illinois licensed day care in my home when my children were young, finishing my degree at Eastern Illinois University with one year toward my Master's Degree in Guidance and Counseling; plus the professional experience of being a caseworker for an Illinois developmentally disabled facility called CCAR; being an Advocate for children with the Illinois Department of Children and Family Services; managing Nancy's Gifts and Cards; having an Illinois and Arizona Real Estate License; working as a volunteer at a local hospital delivering mail and volunteering in the cancer wing; volunteering with the Army Corp of Engineers in Illinois at the visitors center; volunteering with the Port Authority in Florida as a camp host; moving more than twenty-nine times in forty-five years of marriage; working as a paraprofessional in high school; being director of DZ Sorority House; and too many more items to mention. These all helped give me a devout belief in Christian Biblical principles.

My first recollection of hearing God's Word was at the age of five or six at Bible school. On the very last day, the minister invited the children to raise their hands if they wanted Christ to come into their life. I raised my hand. The minister asked if we believed that Jesus died on the cross to save us from sin. He said that God would have mercy on us and forgive us of our sins if we confess them to God in prayer. My life at that point was enlightened with a transformation that will last forever! This transformation can happen for you at any age. All you have to do is believe in God and follow the steps I took. Now, know that you are walking in His light forevermore. Thanks be to God.

My spiritual beliefs tell me that we can become whatever we desire. Too often in counseling, clients are asked to rehash their problems from childhood with the desire to find out where the problem started. However, no one can change the past (Read 2 Corinthians 3:18). No longer must we hide behind a veil of shame. My beliefs caused conflict with the system, and while in college, I began working solely from the positive aspect. I believe the present is where the Lord wants to be with us. He listens. He cares. He forgives us for past mistakes. He answers prayer. Life is simple if we rely on God and live in the here and now with enthusiasm and joy.

ADDITIONAL VERSES FOR AFFIRMATIONS

Affirmation 1: Mark 9:24; John 6:69; John 11:40; John 16:30; Hebrews 11:6

Affirmation 2: Colossians 3:15–16; 1 Revelation 4:9; Hebrews 12:28; 1 Timothy 4:3

Affirmation 3: Philippians 1:3; Romans 1:21; 1 Chronicles 16:4; Psalm 30:12; 1 Timothy 2:1

Affirmation 4: Genesis 32:10; Proverbs 12:4; Matthew 8:8; Luke 15:19; Philippians 1:27

Affirmation 5: Mark 11:24; Philippians 4:6; Colossians 4:2; Mark 11:25; Ephesians 1:18

Affirmation 6: 2 Timothy 1:5; 1 Corinthians 12:4, 7; 1 Peter 4:10; Romans 4:16

Affirmation 7: John 14:27; Romans 2:7; Acts 14:3; Luke 11:13; Acts 15:8

Affirmation 8: Proverbs 10:8; Matthew 5:12; Proverbs 27:11; Acts 13:48; 2 Corinthians 2:2

Affirmation 9: Matthew 4:5; 1 Corinthians 4:3; Hebrews 2:7; Hebrews 13:2; 2 Peter 2:4; Luke 2:9

Affirmation 10: Psalm 6:4; Psalm 103:17; Jeremiah 33:11; Hosea 2:23; John 15:9; Isaiah 63:7

Affirmation 11: Exodus 15:13; Psalm 139:10; John 16:13; Galatians 5:16; Psalm 23:3

Affirmation 12: Romans 7:14; 1 Corinthians 2:14; 1 Corinthians 15:44; Ephesians 5:19; 1 Peter 2:5

Affirmation 13: Matthew 7:22; Mark 6:2; Acts 2:22; Acts 19:11; Galatians 3:5

Affirmation 14: James 3:18; 1 Thessalonians 5:3; Proverbs 14:30; Hebrews 12:11; 1 Timothy 2:2

Affirmation 15: Psalm 119:9; Jeremiah 23:29; Amos 8:13; John 1:1; Ephesians 6:17

Affirmation 16: Hebrews 10:24; Proverbs 11:27; Luke 6:45; Romans 12:2; John 5:42

Affirmation 17: Psalm 108:1; 1 Corinthians 14:26; Psalm 51:14; Psalm 101:1; 2 Samuel 6:21

Affirmation 18: 1 Peter 3:7; John 6:68; John 10:10; Romans 6:23; Psalm 139:24

Affirmation 19: Proverbs 26:20; Psalm 34:4; Deuteronomy 20:8; Acts 27:33; Matthew 6:25

Affirmation 20: Exodus 15:1; Colossians 3:16; Psalm 147:1; Psalm 89:1; 1 Corinthians 14:15

Affirmation 21: Isaiah 42:9; 1 Corinthians 14:39; 1 Corinthians 12:10; Joel 2:28; Acts 2:17

Affirmation 22: Deuteronomy 20:8; Psalm 37:1; Matthew 10:19; Philippians 4:6; Proverbs 12:25

Affirmation 23: 2 Chronicles:19:6; Proverbs 13:16; Proverbs 21:29; Hebrews 10:24; 1 Peter 1:13

Affirmation 24: John 15:14, 17; Deuteronomy 6:24; Genesis 7:5; Joshua 1:9

Affirmation 25: Isaiah 38:17; Psalm 79:9; Act 5:31; Romans 4:7; Luke 24:47

Affirmation 26: Romans 4:5; Daniel 9:9; Jeremiah 31:34; Matthew 26:28; Acts 5:31

Affirmation 27: John 10:9; 1 Corinthians 1:18; Matthew 24:13; Romans 6:23; John 6:68

Affirmation 28: Psalm 1:2; Matthew 22:40; Romans 3:19; Galatians 5:14; Matthew 5:19

Affirmation 29: Psalm 40:8; Hebrews 10:7; 1 Peter 4:2; Proverbs 3:6; Matthew 12:50

Affirmation 30: Psalm 56:3; Psalm 112:7; Proverbs 3:5; Isaiah 26:3; Hebrews 2:13

Affirmation 31: Matthew 9:29; Matthew 17:20; Ephesians 6:16; James 5:15; Luke 7:50

Affirmation 32: This verse stands alone.

Affirmation 33: Proverbs 2:11; Proverbs 18:10; John 17:15

Affirmation 34: Mark 1:15; Acts 16:10; Romans 1:15; 2 Timothy 4:17; Ephesians 6:15

Affirmation 35 Galatians 6:10; Ephesians 2:19; Joshua 24:15; 1 Timothy 3:4; Hebrews 12:28

Affirmation 36: Matthew 22:37; Psalm 103:18; John 14:15; Psalm 119:93; Mark 12:28

Affirmation 37: Psalm 79:8; 1 Corinthians 7:3; Philippians 4:19; Titus 3:14; 2 Corinthians 8:6

Affirmation 38: Psalm 71:17; Luke 13:17; Acts 2:11; Isaiah 25:1; Psalm 145:5

Affirmation 39: Romans 12:8; 2 Corinthians 10:1; Galatians 5:22; Colossians 3:12; 1 Corinthians 13:4

Affirmation 40: 1 Chronicles 16:12; John 12:13; Acts 4:33; Ephesians 3:6; Revelation 7:12

Affirmation 41: John 5:43; 1 Corinthians 13:13; Ephesians 5:25; 1 Peter 4:8; Matthew 19:19

Affirmation 42: Isaiah 63:7; Matthew 5:16; Mark 11:9; Ephesians 1:6; Psalm 144:1

Affirmation 43: Psalm 38:18; Romans 14:11; James 5:16; Mark 1:5; 1 Timothy 6:12

Affirmation 44: Psalm 15:2; Zechariah 8:19; John 15:26; 2 Corinthians 13:8; Ephesians 4:15

Affirmation 45: Mark 11:25; Luke 6:37; Luke 17:4; Psalm 79:9; Hosea 14:2

Affirmation 46: Galatians 5:22; Colossians 3:12; 2 Timothy 3:10; Titus 2:2; 2 Peter 3:15

Affirmation 47: Matthew 22:16; 2 Timothy 4:3; 1 Peter 2:21; Titus 2:7; Hebrews 13:7

Affirmation 48: Philippians 4:6; Matthew 6:2; Acts 20:35; Ephesians 4:28

Affirmation 49: Psalm 36:10; Romans 12:8; 1 Peter 3:11

Affirmation 50: 1 Timothy 5:4; Ephesians 2:19; 1 Timothy 3:12; 2 Peter 1:10; John 15:13

Affirmation 51: Psalm 40:3; Proverbs 3:5; Isaiah 12:2; John 12:46; John 14:1

Affirmation 52: Deuteronomy 28:11; Psalm 41:2; Proverbs 28:25; Psalm 34:12; Daniel 4:27; Micah 4:4

WHAT IS A POSITIVE AFFIRMATION?

Definition: A positive affirmation is a short personal statement in present tense without any negative connotations.

Intent: My hope is that everyone reading this list of positive affirmations will reach positive solutions for life's problems and experience blessings in their life in such a way that their life will begin to honor God.

How to Use These Affirmations

1. Begin and end each day with a prayer about that day's affirmation. Ask God to guide you in how you should use these daily affirmations. God's mercy will open your eyes to new beginnings if you ask.

2. Use this BOOK as a tool to watch your spiritual growth every year. Write as little or as much as you wish in recalling your experiences for the daily journal. Keeping the book open at all times in a place where you can read and reread the Positive Christian Affirmation will help keep it as a daily reminder of your walk with God. It will keep you thinking positive thoughts throughout the day. Each year you will find you have different answers.

3. It is important to first READ, second WRITE DOWN something, and third LOOK AT IT REGULARLY to attain the positive goal.

4. Group study can be in church Sunday School for lessons, at a nursing home as a daily devotional program, at alcohol and drug abuse centers working on positive affirmations, at gamblers anonymous for weekly work toward positive goals, on hospital wards showing ways to overcome depression, etc. These are but a few of the ways this book can be used.

5. This makes a great gift for people recuperating from illness; those who are recently divorced, separated, widowed, or have experienced a death in the family; those suffering from a loss of income or other tragedy; and for those who feel like they are on top of the world with good fortune.

6. The index on pages 4 & 5 will be helpful to ministers or counselors who need to emphasize a specific point such as "patience." Affirmation #46 is "I show patience toward myself and other people." "Forgiven" is in Affirmation #25, which states, "I ask God and I am forgiven for my sins because I belong to Him." Leaving your Positive Christian Affirmation book open to remind you each day, or writing this affirmation even on your mirror in your bathroom will help remind you daily of a positive Christian thought. It takes as little as twenty-one days to change a habit. Let's change from thinking negative thoughts to a positive outlook on the same subject that has been troubling you for hours, days, months, or even years.

7. Learn from reading this book how to write Positive Christian Affirmations, which are short personal statements in present tense without any negative connotations. These Positive Christian Affirmations can be as simple as "I love you," "I love myself," or as complicated as "I am learning daily ways to improve my speech making it more loving, ways to think good thoughts about my job and family, and treating all people with kindness because we are all God's children."

8. Work through this book with your spouse. It is fun to start your day with this book at the breakfast table together as a family. Remember to reward yourself for a job well done after you complete this journey. I personally have a very hard time with people who say negative or harsh things to me. I immediately try to turn it around in my mind thinking how they could have said it in a positive way. I learned how to be positive as a very young person and found out how much better it felt to be positive.

52 Positive Christian Affirmations

(Writing a POSITIVE GOAL and looking at it regularly helps attain that goal.)

1. I believe in God. (John 3:16; Exodus 4:5; Exodus 3:5-6)
2. I am thankful that God chose me as one of His messengers. (1 Timothy 1:12-14; 2 Chronicles 36:16)
3. I Give THANKS in all circumstances. (1 Thessalonians 5:18; Psalm 28:7)
4. Yes, I am worthy and can do everything through Christ. (Philippians 4:13; Romans 16:2)
5. God answered my prayer. (Psalm 20:4-5; 1 Chronicles 5:19-20)
6. Thank You, God, for my wonderful gift of the Holy Spirit. (1 Corinthians 2:12-13; Acts 2:38)
7. I surrender this situation to my Creator. (2 Corinthians 4:8-10; 1 Samuel 23:11)
8. God brought me into the world. I am glad to be alive. (Job 1:21; Psalm 16:9)
9. I know God's angels are guarding me. (Psalm 91:11)
10. LOVE is the greatest gift God gave me. (1 Corinthians 13:2)
11. God's guidance gives me strength. (Psalm 68:35; Exodus 15:2)
12. I continue to grow spiritually. (Acts 2:18; 1 Corinthians 14:37)
13. I see miracles happening around me today. (Acts 2:43; 1 Chronicles 16:11-13)
14. A peaceful life is what I envision now for everyone. (Matthew 5:9; 1 Timothy 2:2)
15. I read God's Word today. (Psalm 119:44-52; Luke 8:21)
16. God works for my good because I love Him. (Romans 8:28; Psalm 57:3)
17. I will sing to the Lord because He has blessed me. (Psalm 13:6; Psalm 98:1)
18. I hold high standards for my life by following Jesus. (Psalm 119:41-43; Matthew 19:28-29)
19. Today, my anxious moment disappeared when I prayed thanking God. (Philippians 4:6; Psalm 139:23)

20. I will sing songs of praise and create ways to celebrate. (Psalm 95:1-3; Psalm 145:7)

21. I know when my intuition is from God. (2 Peter 1:19-21; Job 36:2)

22. I am free from worry. (Matthew 6:25-27; Luke 12:26)

23. I know the power of positive thinking. (1 Timothy 1:18-19; Acts 1:7-8)

24. I obey God's commands and He loves me. (John 14:21; Psalm 119:33-35)

25. I ask God and I am forgiven for my sins because I belong to Him. (Psalm 32:4-5; Acts 2:38)

26. Others are forgiven for their sins when they ask God because they belong to Him. (Psalm 32:1-2)

27. Christ Jesus saved me by His mercy so I would have eternal life. (1 Timothy 1:15-16)

28. It is my pleasure to follow God's law closely with God's people. (Psalm 1:1-2; Psalm 119:42-43)

29. I make good decisions with God's help doing God's will. (Hebrews 13:20-21; 1 Thessalonians 5:18)

30. I continue to trust in God. (Proverbs 16:20; John 14:1)

31. When God closes one door for me, He always opens a better door. (Hebrews 11:1-3; James 4-10; Psalm 118:19-24)

32. When any two or more Christians ask God's blessing on anything God will do it. (Matthew 18:19)

33. I am safe at all times. (Psalm 31:14-19; Proverbs 1:33; John 5:18; Psalm 4:8)

34. The Good News about the Kingdom of God is being preached throughout the world. (Matthew 24:14; Luke16:16)

35. I am thankful I am a part of the universal family of God. (Acts 2:39)

36. I obey God's commandments. (Deuteronomy 5:11-22; Matthew 19:17-19)

37. God gives me everything I need. (1 Corinthians 3:21-23; Matthew 6:8)

38. Wonderful people and situations surround me now. (1 Corinthians 5:11-12; 1 Peter 2:9)

39. I show kindness and thoughtfulness to other people. (Proverbs 11:17; Jeremiah 9:24)

40. I remember one blessing after another. (John 1:16; Isaiah 12:2)

41. I love everyone. (Matthew 43-44; 1 John 4:7)

42. I continue to praise God. (Hebrews 13:15; Revelation 19:5)

43. I confess my sins to God and marvel at His miracles. (Job 5:8-9; 1 John 1:9)

44. I speak the truth with loving expression. (Deuteronomy 5:20; Zechariah 8:16)

45. Forgiving others and myself helps ME. (Matthew 6:14-15; Ephesians 4:32)

46. I show patience toward other people and myself. (Proverbs 25:15; Colossians 1:11)

47. Teaching and being a good example for the youth of today is important to me. (Proverbs 22:6; Matthew 19:14-15)

48. Being a balanced person means taking care of my needs and others' needs regularly. (James 2:14-17; Proverbs 11:24-25; Romans 12:8)

49. I align myself with loving, kind, and peaceful people. (Hebrews 12:14; Romans 14:17-19; 2 Corinthians 13:11; Isaiah 32:18)

50. Today, my goal is to bring positive energy to my home, work, and friends. (Colossians 3:12; Genesis 14-16)

51. Breathing deeply while trusting God keeps me healthy, happy, and joyous. (Psalm 5:11; 2 Samuel 7:28)
52. I am well supplied for today and all of my tomorrows. (Proverbs 8:18-21)

All of these affirmations are my personal interpretations. They have been very powerful for my life.

If anything does not feel right for you, simply read the listed Scripture everyday and record your journal for that day according to your positive statements.

AFFIRMATION # 1

I believe in God. (John 3:16; Exodus 4:5; Exodus 3:5-6)

Monday
1. Tell your story after reading any one of the Bible verses listed for each day of the week. Additional verses on page 11 and 12.

Tuesday
2.

Wednesday
3.

Thursday

4.

POSITIVE

Friday

5

.

Saturday

6.

Sunday

7. Write a letter to God and tell Him about your belief in Him. Say a prayer thanking God for all you have. Tell Him how much you believe in Him and love Him.

AFFIRMATION # 2

I Am Thankful That God Chose Me as One of His Messengers. (1 Timothy 1:12-14; 2 Chronicles 36-16)

Monday
1. Tell your story after reading any one of the Bible verses listed for each day of the week. Additional verses on page 11 and 12.

Tuesday
2.

Wednesday
3.

Thursday

4.

MESSENGER

Friday

5.

Saturday

6.

.

Sunday

7. Write what you feel is the most important message God wants you to convey to people. Say a prayer asking God to lead you.

AFFIRMATION # 3

I Give Thanks in All Circumstances. (1 Thessalonians 5:18; Psalm 28:7)

Monday
1. Tell your story after reading any one of the Bible verses listed for each day of the week. Additional verses on page 11 and 12.

Tuesday
2.

Wednesday
3.

Thursday

4.

THANKFUL

Friday

5.

Saturday

6.

Sunday

7. Pray this prayer: "Heavenly Father, thank You for everything I have. You, I believe in, trust and obey. I listen for Your voice when I meditate on You throughout the day. Show me Your ways, Lord. Amen." Now sit quietly with eyes closed for five minutes. Write what else comes to mind.

AFFIRMATION # 4

Yes, I Am Worthy and Can Do Everything Through Christ. (Philippians 4:13; Romans 16:2)

Monday
1. Tell your story after reading any one of the Bible verses listed for each day of the week. Additional verses on page 11 and 12.

Tuesday
2.

Wednesday
3.

Thursday

4.

WORTHY

Friday

5.

Saturday

6.

Sunday

7. Say a prayer every time you know you were God's helper today. Write them down here.

AFFIRMATION # 5

God Answered My Prayer.   (Psalm 20:4-5)

Monday
1. Tell your story after reading any one of the Bible verses listed for each day of the week. Additional verses on page 11 and 12.

Tuesday
2.

Wednesday
3.

Thursday

4.

PRAYER

Friday

5.

Saturday

6.

Sunday

7. God does not answer all our prayers because we do not know what is best. Write a prayer to thank God telling Him that you know He wants only what is best for you.

AFFIRMATION #6

Thank You, God, for My Wonderful Gift of the Holy Spirit. (Acts 2:38; 1 Corinthians 2:12-13)

Monday

1. Tell your story after reading any one of the Bible verses listed for each day of the week. Additional verses on page 11 and 12.

Tuesday

2.

Wednesday

3.

Thursday

4.

GIFTS

Friday

5.

Saturday

6.

Sunday

7. Write a prayer to thank God asking Him to help you with the gifts He gave you.

AFFIRMATION #7

I Surrender This Situation to My Creator. (2 Corinthians 4:8-10; 1 Samuel 23:11)

Monday
1. Tell your story after reading any one of the Bible verses listed for each day of the week. Additional verses on page 11 and 12.

Tuesday
2.

Wednesday
3.

Thursday

4.

SURRENDER

Friday

5.

Saturday

6.

Sunday

7. Now tell how relaxed and relieved you feel after giving a situation to God with no plans to take it back. Pray now asking God to handle it. Thank God for His help.

AFFIRMATION # 8

God Brought Me Into the World. I Am Glad to be Alive. (Job 1:21; Psalm 16:9)

Monday
1. Tell your story after reading any one of the Bible verses listed for each day of the week. Additional verses on page 11 and 12.

Tuesday
2.

Wednesday
3.

Thursday

4.

HAPPINESS

Friday

5.

Saturday

6.

Sunday

7. Now go out and show the world you are GLAD TO BE ALIVE. How can you do this? Write down a prayer for help from your Heavenly Father thanking Him for your life.

AFFIRMATION #9

I Know God's Angels are Guarding Me. (Psalm 91:11)

Monday
1. Tell your story after reading any one of the Bible verses listed for each day of the week. Additional verses on page 11 and 12.

Tuesday
2.

Wednesday
3.

Thursday

4.

ANGELS

Friday

5.

Saturday

6.

Sunday

7. Write a prayer thanking God for providing angels to guard you and to keep you safe.

AFFIRMATION # 10

LOVE is the Greatest Gift God Gave Me. (1 Corinthians 13:2)

Monday
1. Tell your story after reading any one of the Bible verses listed for each day of the week. Additional verses on page 11 and 12.

Tuesday
2.

Wednesday
3.

41

Thursday

4.

LOVE

Friday

5.

Saturday

6.

Sunday

7. Accepting and giving LOVE is powerful. Pray now for God to show you how to give and accept LOVE the way HE wants you to. Complete this prayer: "Dear Lord, teach me to Love and accept Love daily, hourly, and every minute. Your Love for us is so powerful. I want to (finish this prayer in your own words)."

AFFIRMATION # 11

God's Guidance Gives Me Strength. (Psalm 68:35; Exodus 15:2)

Monday
1. Tell your story after reading any one of the Bible verses listed for each day of the week. Additional verses on page 11 and 12.

Tuesday
2.

Wednesday
3.

Thursday

4.

GOD'S GUIDANCE

Friday

5.

Saturday

6.

Sunday

7. Write your prayer thanking God for His guidance and strength. God will not leave you. When you know God and talk to Him daily, He will be there in times of need. God may handle the situation entirely or He may want you to do something. Listen.

AFFIRMATION # 12

I Continue to Grow Spiritually. (Acts 2:18; 1 Corinthians 14:37)

Monday

1. Tell your story after reading any one of the Bible verses listed for each day of the week. Additional verses on page 11 and 12.

Tuesday

2.

Wednesday

3.

Thursday

4.

SPIRITUAL GROWTH

Friday

5.

Saturday

6.

Sunday

7. In helping others, we help ourselves. Write a prayer for continued spiritual growth. Remember to pray a prayer of thanksgiving for all God is doing for you and others.

AFFIRMATION # 13

I See Miracles Happening Around Me Today. (Acts 2:43, 1 Chronicles 16:11-13)

Monday
1. Tell your story after reading any one of the Bible verses listed for each day of the week. Additional verses on page 11 and 12.

Tuesday
2.

Wednesday
3.

Thursday

4.

MIRACLES

Friday

5.

Saturday

6.

Sunday

7. Sometimes God may be saying to us to change the situation. Ask God how or if you can indeed cause a change that will allow a miracle to happen. Sometimes God is the miracle. Sometimes He alone makes the miracle happen. Now envision and pray for the miracle you need. Thank God for His answering your prayer even though it has not happened yet.

AFFIRMATION # 14

A Peaceful Life is What I Envision Now for Everyone. (Matthew 5:9; 1 Timothy 2:2)

Monday
1. Tell your story after reading any one of the Bible verses listed for each day of the week. Additional verses on page 11 and 12.

Tuesday
2.

Wednesday
3.

49

Thursday

4.

PEACEFUL

Friday

5.

Saturday

6.

Sunday

7. Write a prayer for PEACE throughout the world. Place it on your mirror to read every morning. Ask at least five (5) people to pray for the same thing everyday.

AFFIRMATION # 15

I Read God's Word in My Bible Today. (Psalm 119: 44-52; Luke 8:21)

Monday
1. Tell your story after reading any one of the Bible verses listed for each day of the week. Additional verses on page 11 and 12.

Tuesday
2.

Wednesday
3.

Thursday

4.

REGULAR BIBLE READING

Friday

5.

Saturday

6.

Sunday

7. When we explain to people how much help reading the Bible is for us, it encourages others to do the same. Write a prayer asking God to lead you into conversations that will help others grow through Bible reading. Thank Him for always listening.

AFFIRMATION # 16

God Works For My Good Because I Love Him. (Romans 8:28; Psalm 57:3)

Monday
1. Tell your story after reading any one of the Bible verses listed for each day of the week. Additional verses on page 11 and 12.

Tuesday
2.

Wednesday
3.

Thursday

4.

I LOVE GOD

Friday

5.

Saturday

6.

Sunday

7. Write a prayer asking God to continue bringing "good" into your life because you love Him. Start the prayer this way: Lord God, it is YOU I love. I thank You for bringing so much GOOD into my life. I thank You for... (Finish this prayer in your own words.)

AFFIRMATION # 17

I will Sing to the Lord Because He has Blessed Me. (Psalm 13:6; Psalm 98:1)

Monday
1. Tell your story after reading any one of the Bible verses listed for each day of the week.
    Additional verses on page 11 and 12.

Tuesday
2.

Wednesday
3.

Thursday

4.

SING

Friday

5.

Saturday

6.

Sunday

7. What does singing and praising God in church mean to you? Explain the blessings and praises in prayer. Remember in all prayers to be thankful to the Holy One.

AFFIRMATION # 18

I Hold High Standards for My Life by Setting Positive Goals. (Psalm 119:41-43; Matthew 19:28-29)

Monday
1. Tell your story after reading any one of the Bible verses listed for each day of the week. Additional verses on page 11 and 12.

Tuesday
2.

Wednesday
3.

Thursday

4.

POSITIVE GOALS

Friday

5.

Saturday

6.

Sunday

7. Write a prayer and speak positive words. Ask for specific things and be thankful.

AFFIRMATION # 19

Today My Anxious Moment Disappeared When I Prayed Thanking God. (Philippians 4:6; Psalm 139:23)

Monday
1. Tell your story after reading any one of the Bible verses listed for each day of the week. Additional verses on page 11 and 12.

Tuesday
2.

Wednesday
3.

Thursday

4.

PRAY

Friday

5.

Saturday

6.

Sunday

7. God has a divine plan. Write a prayer asking for His divine plan to show you the way to be thankful for the most difficult part of your past. You can start living today. The here and now is great. Live life in joy, happiness, singing, smiling, and be the Christian that is pleasing to God. Leave the past in the past and forgive. The future is yet to come.

AFFIRMATION # 20

I will Sing Songs of Praise and Create Ways to Celebrate. (Psalm 95:1-3; Psalm 145:7)

Monday
1. Tell your story after reading any one of the Bible verses listed for each day of the week. Additional verses on page 11 and 12.

Tuesday
2.

Wednesday
3.

Thursday

4.

CELEBRATE

Friday

5.

Saturday

6.

Sunday

7. Pray this prayer: Heavenly Father, please remind me to be a joyous person. I praise You. Teach me to celebrate by praising You daily with my family and friends. Make me a happy person starting now and forever more. (Finish this prayer in your own words.) Thank you Lord. Amen.

AFFIRMATION # 21

I know when My Intuition is From God. (2 Peter 1:19-21; Job 36:2)

Monday

1. Tell your story after reading any one of the Bible verses listed for each day of the week. Additional verses on page 11 and 12.

Tuesday

2.

Wednesday

3.

Thursday

4.

INSPIRED BY GOD

Friday

5.

Saturday

6.

Sunday

7. Write a prayer now asking and thanking God for showing you the way He wants you to go today. Ask Him to take you step-by-step throughout this day and forevermore.

AFFIRMATION # 22

I Am Free From Worry. (Matthew 6:25-27; Luke 12:26)

Monday
1. Tell your story after reading any one of the Bible verses listed for each day of the week. Additional verses on page 11 and 12.

Tuesday
2.

Wednesday
3.

Thursday

4.

FREE FROM WORRY

Friday

5.

Saturday

6.

Sunday

7. Write a prayer that will help you turn to God the very second you begin to worry. Then, thank Him for taking all the worry away. You are now so relieved with God's help.

AFFIRMATION # 23

I Know the Power of Positive Thinking. (1 Timothy 1:18-19; Acts 1:7-8)

Monday
1. Tell your story after reading any one of the Bible verses listed for each day of the week. Additional verses on page 11 and 12.

Tuesday
2.

Wednesday
3.

Thursday

4.

POSITIVE THINKING

Friday

5.

Saturday

6.

Sunday

7. If you have difficulty thinking and writing in a positive way, put a note on your mirror to remind you to BE A POSITIVE PERSON with God's help. Write a prayer to cover this situation.

AFFIRMATION # 24

I Obey God's commands and tell myself, "He loves me." (John 14:21; Psalm 119:33-35)

Monday
1. Tell your story after reading any one of the Bible verses listed for each day of the week. Additional verses on page 11 and 12.

Tuesday
2.

Wednesday
3.

Thursday

4.

OBEY

Friday

5.

Saturday

6.

Sunday

7. Think about things you have overlooked lately. You now want to obey God in this prayer. Write the prayer. Tell Him you know He loves you and you love Him.   Finish the prayer in your own words. Thank Him for His help.

AFFIRMATION # 25

I Ask God and I Am Forgiven for My Sins Because I Belong to Him. (Psalm 32:4-5; Acts 2:38)

Monday
1. Tell your story after reading any one of the Bible verses listed for each day of the week. Additional verses on page 11 and 12.

Tuesday
2.

Wednesday
3.

Thursday

4.

FORGIVEN

Friday

5.

Saturday

6.

Sunday

7. Write a prayer knowing that you are already forgiven. Thank God for that forgiveness before closing your prayer. After the prayer, celebrate and be happy!

AFFIRMATION # 26

Other people are Forgiven for Their Sins When They Ask God. (Psalm 32:1-2)

Monday
1. Tell your story after reading any one of the Bible verses listed for each day of the week. Additional verses on page 11 and 12.

Tuesday
2.

Wednesday
3.

Thursday

4.

FORGIVENESS

Friday

5.

Saturday

6.

Sunday

7. Write a prayer saying WE ALL MAKE MISTAKES. Thank God for forgiveness. Now, leave it all in God's hands.

AFFIRMATION # 27

Christ Jesus Saved Me By His Mercy so I Would Have Eternal Life. (I Timothy 1:15-16)

Monday
1. Tell your story after reading any one of the Bible verses listed for each day of the week.
   Additional verses on page 11 and 12.

Tuesday
2.

Wednesday
3.

75

Thursday

4.

MERCY

Friday

5.

Saturday

6.

Sunday

7. God wants us to love even ourselves. Write a prayer thanking God for that.

AFFIRMATION # 28

It is My Pleasure to Follow God More Closely with Positive God-Like People. (Psalm 1:12; Psalm 119:42-43)

Monday
1. Tell your story after reading any one of the Bible verses listed for each day of the week.
   Additional verses on page 11 and 12.

Tuesday
2.

Wednesday
3.

Thursday

4.

POSITIVE

Friday

5.

Saturday

6.

Sunday

7. Delight in doing everything God wants you to do. Write a prayer starting like this: Heavenly Father, I want to follow You more closely. I want to meditate and hear Your words. Keep me safe from harmful people. End by thanking God for His leadership.

AFFIRMATION # 29

I Make Good Decisions with God's Help Doing God's Will. (Hebrews 13:20-21; 1 Thessalonians 5:18)

Monday
1. Tell your story after reading any one of the Bible verses listed for each day of the week. Additional verses on page 11 and 12.

Tuesday
2.

Wednesday
3.

Thursday

4.

GOD'S WILL

Friday

5.

Saturday

6.

Sunday

7. Write a prayer asking the Lord to equip you with all you need to do His will. This is an agreement between God and you, signed in His blood following the great Shepherd all the days of your life. End with "to God be the Glory forever. Amen."

AFFIRMATION # 30

I Continue to Trust in God. (Proverbs 16:20; John 14:1)

      Monday
1. Tell your story after reading any one of the Bible verses listed for each day of the week. Additional verses on page 11 and 12.

      Tuesday
2.

      Wednesday
3.

Thursday

4.

TRUST

Friday

5.

Saturday

6.

Sunday

7. My prayer is that all those who do not know God will find Him and trust in Him. We are unable to know the difference until seeing someone begin to notice the light of Christ. Write a prayer so everyone in the world will know God, trust God, and be thankful to God.

AFFIRMATION # 31

When God Closes One Door For Me, He Always Opens a Better Door. (Hebrews 11:1-3; James 4:10; Psalm 118:19-24)

Monday
1. Tell your story after reading any one of the Bible verses listed for each day of the week. Additional verses on page 11 and 12.

Tuesday
2.

Wednesday
3.

Thursday

4.

BETTER DOORS OPEN

Friday

5.

Saturday

6.

Sunday

7. Write a prayer thanking God for your faith. Ask Him to always open better doors.

AFFIRMATION # 32

When any Two or More Christians ask God's Blessing on Anything, God Will Do it for You. (Matthew 18:19)

Monday
1. Tell your story after reading any one of the Bible verses listed for each day of the week. Additional verses on page 11 and 12.

Tuesday
2.

Wednesday
3.

Thursday

4.

GOD'S BLESSING

Friday

5.

Saturday

6.

Sunday

7. Write a prayer asking for your prayer to be answered because we are Yours, Lord, and You are with us. Heavenly Father, we pray. End the prayer thanking God for that blessing even though the results are yet to come.

AFFIRMATION #33

I am safe at all times. (Psalm 31:14-19; John 5:18; Proverbs 1:33)

Monday
1. Tell your story after reading any one of the Bible verses listed for each day of the week. Additional verses on page 11 and 12.

Tuesday
2.

Wednesday
3.

Thursday

4.

SAFE

Friday

5.

Saturday

6.

Sunday

7. Write a thankful prayer for the knowledge that God protects His people.

AFFIRMATION # 34

The Good News about the Kingdom is Being Preached Throughout the World. (Matthew 24:14; Luke 16:16)

Monday
1. Tell your story after reading any one of the Bible verses listed for each day of the week. Additional verses on page 11 and 12.

Tuesday
2.

Wednesday
3.

Thursday

4.

CHRIST IS THE GOOD NEWS

Friday

5.

Saturday

6.

Sunday

7. Write the ending to this prayer: Heavenly Father, help me to realize those close to me who need encouragement about the Gospel. Assist me today and in the years to come in helping more people come closer to You. For those who have not experienced God… (Now, finish this prayer in your own words).

AFFIRMATION # 35

I Am Thankful I Am a Part of the Universal Family of God. (Acts 2:39)

Monday
1. Tell your story after reading any one of the Bible verses listed for each day of the week. Additional verses on page 11 and 12.

Tuesday
2.

Wednesday
3.

Thursday

4.

HOLY SPIRIT

Friday

5.

Saturday

6.

Sunday

7. Write a prayer for those who have strayed from God, but have returned to Him. End with a thank you for all of this and more.

AFFIRMATION # 36

I Obey God's Commandments. (Deuteronomy 5:11-22; Matthew 19: 17-19)

Monday
1. Tell your story after reading any one of the Bible verses listed for each day of the week.
   Additional verses on page 11 and 12.

Tuesday
2.

Wednesday
3.

Thursday

4.

10 COMMANDMENTS

Friday

5.

Saturday

6.

Sunday

7. In writing this prayer, include others you love and those who do not like to make right decisions. Thank God for leading us on the right path.

AFFIRMATION #37

God Gives Me Everything I Need. (1 Corinthians 3:21-23; Matthew 6:8)

Monday
1. Tell your story after reading any one of the Bible verses listed for each day of the week. Additional verses on page 11 and 12.

Tuesday
2.

Wednesday
3.

Thursday

4.

HEAVEN

Friday

5.

Saturday

6.

Sunday

7. Make a list of things that you would take with you in a car if you had to evacuate. Say a prayer thanking God for supplying us with what we really need and some items that we want. You are so lucky to have something. As you know, many people have nothing. Homeless people are very abundant in all states and countries.

AFFIRMATION #38

Wonderful People and Situations Surround Me Now. (1 Corinthians 5:11-12; 1 Peter 2:9)

Monday
1. Tell your story after reading any one of the Bible verses listed for each day of the week.
   Additional verses on page 11 and 12.

Tuesday
2.

Wednesday
3.

Thursday

4.

FRIENDS

Friday

5.

Saturday

6.

Sunday

7.   No one is perfect. This deals with sinful actions. Write a prayer asking for God's help with your actions. Make sure family and friends know you love them in your prayer. End by thanking God for wonderful people and situations that surround you.

AFFIRMATION # 39

I show Kindness and Thoughtfulness to Other People. (Proverbs 11:17; Jeremiah 9:24)

Monday
1. Tell your story after reading any one of the Bible verses listed for each day of the week. Additional verses on page 11 and 12.

Tuesday
2.

Wednesday
3.

Thursday

4.

KINDNESS

Friday

5.

Saturday

6.

Sunday

7. Write a prayer that will promote kindness in your world. End by thanking God for all the kind and thoughtful people who make up this world.

AFFIRMATION #40

When I Close My Eyes and Trust in God, I remember one blessing after another.   (John 1:16; Isaiah 12:2)

Monday
1. Tell your story after reading any one of the Bible verses listed for each day of the week. Additional verses on page 11 and 12.

Tuesday
2.

Wednesday
3.

Thursday

4.

GOD

Friday

5.

Saturday

6.

Sunday

7. Write a prayer for the wonderful care that God gives us when trusting in Him. End with thanking Him for being able to relax in His loving arms.

AFFIRMATION # 41

I Love Everyone. (Matthew 5:44; 1 John 4:7)

Monday
1. Tell your story after reading any one of the Bible verses listed for each day of the week.
   Additional verses on page 11 and 12.

Tuesday
2.

Wednesday
3.

Thursday

4.

LOVE

Friday

5.

Saturday

6.

Sunday

7. Write your prayer asking God to help you LOVE everyone. God shows us in this way how very much He loves us. We need to give thanks to God for His unfailing love.

AFFIRMATION #42

I Continue to Praise God. (Hebrews 13:15; Revelation 19:5)

Monday

1. Tell your story after reading any one of the Bible verses listed for each day of the week. Additional verses on page 11 and 12.

Tuesday

2.

Wednesday

3.

Thursday

4.

PRAISE

Friday

5.

Saturday

6.

Sunday

7. Write a prayer that is worthy of being placed on your refrigerator for the rest of the year as to how much you praise God. Thank Him for daily walking with you.

AFFIRMATION #43

I Confess My Sins to God and Marvel at His Miracles. (Job 5:8-9; 1 John 1:9)

Monday
1. Tell your story after reading any one of the Bible verses listed for each day of the week. Additional verses on page 11 and 12.

Tuesday
2.

Wednesday
3.

Thursday

4.

MIRACLES

Friday

5.

Saturday

6.

Sunday

7. Write a prayer confessing any sins you want forgiven. Also, thank God for the desire to want to always lay your sins at His feet. Watch how much less you sin. Watch for the MIRACLES!

AFFIRMATION #44

I Speak the Truth with Loving Expression. (Deuteronomy 5:20; Zechariah 8:16)

Monday
1. Tell your story after reading any one of the Bible verses listed for each day of the week. Additional verses on page 11 and 12.

Tuesday
2.

Wednesday
3.

Thursday

4.

TRUTH

Friday

5.

Saturday

6.

Sunday

7. Write your prayer about never lying again. Thank God for listening and helping.

AFFIRMATION #45

Forgiving Other People and Myself helps Me. (Matthew 6:14-15; Ephesians 4:32)

Monday
1. Tell your story after reading any one of the Bible verses listed for each day of the week.
   Additional verses on page 11 and 12.

Tuesday
2.

Wednesday
3.

Thursday

4.

FORGIVENESS

Friday

5.

Saturday

6.

Sunday

7. Write a prayer asking God to help you forgive others easily or instantly so you will feel good about yourself and them. Thank Him for His help. (If you do not forgive easily, put this prayer on your mirror in your bathroom to remind you daily.)

AFFIRMATION #46

I Show Patience toward Myself and Other People. (Proverbs 25:15; Colossians 1:11)

Monday
1. Tell your story after reading any one of the Bible verses listed for each day of the week. Additional verses on page 11 and 12.

Tuesday
2.

Wednesday
3.

Thursday

4.

PATIENCE

Friday

5.

Saturday

6.

Sunday

7. Write a prayer for patience throughout the UNIVERSE. Trying times test our patience. Pray for peace. Pray for the leaders of all countries to use patience and a soft tongue to lead us with God's assistance. Finish this prayer with, "Thank You, Lord, for all of this and more." Put this on your refrigerator and read it often.

AFFIRMATION #47

Teaching and Being a Good Example for the Youth of Today is Important To Me. (Proverbs 22:6; Matthew 19:14-15)

Monday
1. Tell your story after reading any one of the Bible verses listed for each day of the week. Additional verses on page 11 and 12.

Tuesday
2.

Wednesday
3.

Thursday

4.

TEACHING OTHERS

Friday

5.

Saturday

6.

Sunday

7. Write a prayer to forgive yourself for sometimes taking the wrong path, thanking God for guiding you onto the right path during your youth and at any stage of life that is very important to your Christian walk. Ask God to show you the best way to teach youth about Him. Write that prayer now.

AFFIRMATION #48

Being a Balanced Person Means Taking Care of My Needs and Others' Needs Regularly.
(James 2:14-17; Proverbs 11:24-25; Romans 12:8)

Monday
1. Tell your story after reading any one of the Bible verses listed for each day of the week.
   Additional verses on page 11 and 12.

Tuesday
2.

Wednesday
3.

Thursday

4.

BALANCE

Friday

5.

Saturday

6.

Sunday

7. Write a prayer thanking God for all you have. Thank Him for the things that you are able to share with others, giving freely. Let those you share with know that it is given with God's blessing. Finish this prayer in your own words.

AFFIRMATION #49

I Align Myself With Loving, Kind, and Peaceful People. (Hebrews 12:14; Romans 14:17-19; 2 Corinthians 13:11; Isaiah 32:18)

Monday
1. Tell your story after reading any one of the Bible verses listed for each day of the week.
    Additional verses on page 11 and 12.

Tuesday
2.

Wednesday
3.

Thursday

4.

LOVING

Friday

5.

Saturday

6.

Sunday

7. Write a prayer to treasure the loving, kind, and peaceful friends you have. Ask God's forgiveness and ask Him to help you be a good example of these characteristics. Pray for those who do not exhibit these traits that they will see the error of their ways. Thank God that you know the difference in loving and unloving, kind and unkind, peaceful and not peaceful. Ask that the whole world sees these differences and strives for God's peaceful ways.

AFFIRMATION #50

Today My Goal is to Bring Positive Energy to My Home, Work, and Friends. (Colossians 3:12; Genesis 14-16)

Monday
1. Tell your story after reading any one of the Bible verses listed for each day of the week. Additional verses on page 11 and 12.

Tuesday
2.

Wednesday
3.

Thursday

4.

PEACE

Friday

5.

Saturday

6.

Sunday

7. Write a prayer for world peace to become a reality.

AFFIRMATION #51

Breathing Deeply while Trusting God Keeps Me Healthy, Happy, and Joyous. (Psalm 5:11; 2 Samuel 7:28)

Monday
1. Tell your story after reading any one of the Bible verses listed for each day of the week. Additional verses on page 11 and 12.

Tuesday
2.

Wednesday
3.

Thursday

4.

TRUSTING GOD

Friday

5.

Saturday

6.

Sunday

7. Write a prayer for good health, happiness, and joy. Thank God for these.

AFFIRMATION #52

I Am Well Supplied for Today and All of My Tomorrows. (Proverbs 8:18-21)

Monday
1. Tell your story after reading any one of the Bible verses listed for each day of the week. Additional verses on page 11 and 12.

Tuesday
2.

Wednesday
3.

Thursday

4.

FAITH

Friday

5.

Saturday

6.

Sunday

7. Write a prayer asking the Lord to forgive you of all your known and unknown sins. Ask to receive God's gifts more abundantly now knowing He alone is your supplier. Thank Him for all He has done for you in the past.

CONCLUSION

THIS CONCLUDES THE POSITIVE CHRISTIAN AFFIRMATIONS. PURCHASE A NEW BOOK EACH YEAR TO COMPARE YOUR ANSWERS AND WATCH YOUR SPIRITUAL GROWTH. MAY GOD BLESS YOUR POSITIVE JOURNEY IN LIFE!

How to Use this Book

a. Beginning and ending with a prayer asking for God's guidance is the way to use daily affirmations. God's mercy will open our eyes to new beginnings if we ask.

b. It is through reading, writing down a POSITIVE GOAL, and looking at the affirmation regularly that will help to establish a new habit.

c. In a group study: each person can pick one affirmation and read their affirmation for a sharing of experiences. When negative words are said, cancel them with a positive phrase. Become aware of how to change with positive thoughts and words.

d. This book will help you watch your spiritual growth every year. Purchase this book for as many years as you want to check the previous year's answers for comparison. Continue rereading and studying for many years. Each year you will find you have different answers due to your spiritual growth.

AFFIRMATION INDEX

Prayer (#5)
Preached (#34)
Read (#15)
Regularly (#48)
Relaxation (#40)
Safe (#33)
Sing (#17, 20)
Sins (#25, 26, #43)
Speak (#44)
Spiritually (#12)
Strength (#11)
Surrender (#7)
Teaching (#47)
Thankful (#2, 35), thanked (#19), thanks (#3, 6)
Thoughtful (#39)
Today (#13, 15, 18, 19, 47, 50, 52) now (#14, 38)
Trusting God (#51), trust (#30, 40)
Truth (#44)
Universal family of God (#35)
Well supplied (#52)
Wonderful (#38)
World (#34)
Worry (#22)
Worthy (#4)
Youth (#47)

THANK YOU

THANK YOU FOR PURCHASING THIS BOOK. I HOPE YOU HAVE ENJOYED YOUR SPIRITUAL GROWTH THROUGHOUT THIS TIME.

PASS IT ON TO YOUR CHURCH, FAMILY, AND FRIENDS.

MAY GOD'S BLESSINGS BE ON THIS MATERIAL AND ITS READERS!

Made in the USA
Monee, IL
23 July 2021